Menorca Travel Guide

Sightseeing, Hotel, Restaurant & Shopping Highlights

Amanda Morgan

Table of Contents

Menorca

Menorca (also known as Minorca) is one of the most beautiful islands in the Mediterranean. One of the Spanish Balearic Islands, Menorca is known for its quiet ambience, golden beaches and sparkling oceans.

This island off the coast of mainland Spain may look just a little bit too laid back, but this is a mischaracterisation and you will find a wealth of activities and interesting places to keep even the most demanding tourist happy.

Indeed, the vibe is far more relaxed than other commercial islands, and this grants you the opportunity to indulge in all your favorite activities at leisure.

It is a popular destination among sporting types and boasts some of the best diving spots in the entire Mediterranean. The island is dotted with secret areas and sheltered coves that play home to the nightingales. Their fabled songs can be heard echoing through the island in the warm spring and summer months. It is of little wonder that Menorca is quickly gaining popularity as the destination for young couples and families.

When coming to Menorca, visitors seek sun, sea and sand, and the island will not disappoint. An ancient city is surrounded and cradled by imposing cliffs, white beaches, sweeping fields and woody ravines. This jewel of the Balearic Islands is a place of contrast, of remote beaches and vibrant city life, of relaxing and indulging.

Menorca's greatest appeal lies in its beaches, with over 100 beaches to choose from. Nude bathing is still commonplace at many beaches, but the practice thereof is technically illegal. Going for the pleasant weather, hearty food and beaches alone is reason enough to visit Menorca. However, it is its rich heritage and ancient history of a lifetime of invasions that invites travelers to explore its secrets.

Commanding one of the best and strategic natural harbour positions this side of the Med, people settled on the island as early as 4000BC. Thanks to this strategic and popular position, Menorca has seen its fair share of upheaval.

The first inhabitants are believed to Spaniards from the Neolithic era, and their decedents build the monolithic structures that we see to this day scattered around the island. The island range was furthermore frequented by Barbary Pirates from the Americas, resulting in the many watchtowers and fortifications that are still standing

No doubt these invasions helped to shape the current state of affairs. Modern day Menorca is completely self-sufficient and independent. It does not rely solely on tourism, as it has a booming industry of its own. Hand-made leatherwork, costume jewelry and even locally manufactured gin will make a fine souvenir.

In spite of its increasing popularity, Menorca remains essentially unspoilt, maintaining its Spanish charm and welcoming temperament.

Culture

The richness of the culture is mainly due to the said strategic and central position of the island in the heart of the Med. Traditions were greatly shaped by the invasions and colonisations since explores first discovered its shores.

Locals speak a dialect of Catalan, a colorful language that has its roots in Arab and French, with a British influence. In contrast, the architecture is strongly Moor inspired, as can be seen in the white washed houses and complicated cistern systems.

As is customary in a predominantly Spanish culture, warm hospitality and chivalry is at the order of the day, and it is very common to acknowledge and greet the people you meet. And best not forget about the time honoured custom of the midday siesta that is still practiced in many areas. Locals are a jovial bunch, and this afternoon nap enables them to fully enjoy their evenings. Here, people will rarely dine out before 10.00pm.

Dating back to the times of the invasions, landowners kept Berber horses in order to defend the island from invaders, and these strong equestrian traditions are observed all over the island. Menorcans are fiercely proud of their powerful and spirited horses, famed for their beauty and speed. Races are a favourite pastime of many, with weekly events and fiesta taking place is both Ciutadella and Mao.

Locals love a good merrymaking, paired with a passion for concocting simple but scrumptious culinary delights. Most of the dishes are prepared from local ingredients, with a strong focus on seafood, cheese and locally produced fresh produce. You might say that gin is the national drink, as it is distilled on the island from grapes, and flavoured with juniper.

Location & Orientation

The island is located right in the heart of the western Mediterranean of the West Coast of Spain, but lies almost halfway between Marseille in France, and Algiers in Algeria.

Menorca is also referred to as "The Quiet One" out of the Balearic Islands, as party goers tend to favour the neighbouring island of Ibiza. With a current population of roughly 68 000 inhabitants, Menorca has undergone very little commercial changes. It has resisted full-blown urbanization and kept itself sheltered from the effects that come with mass development.

Still, it is the second largest island the Balearic range, but with more beaches than Majorca and Ibiza put together, and with 216 kilometers of pristine coastline, it is hardly surprising. Menorca covers a total area of 700 square kilometres, with only 47 kilometers between the main towns of Ciutadella and Mao.

Es Castell is the last town on the far eastern side, and is the first to see the sun rise. The capital of Mahon (also called Mao) is also located on the eastern side, overlooking the infamous port from a great rocky outcrop. In contrast, the northern part is rugged and rocky, with small red beach and stark cliff faces. Sparse vegetation here is encouraged by the powerful Tramuntana wind.

Climate & When to Visit

Menorca enjoys a temperate climate throughout the year thanks mostly to its proximity to the Med. The weather is classically warm and dry during summer, with roughly 300 days of sunshine per year, and mild winters.

The average temperature usually remains at a very agreeable 17 degrees Celsius, but can climb well into the thirties in mid-summer months. Thankfully, the cooling sea breeze will see that you are never uncomfortably hot for too long. The summer months from June to September sees little to no rain, whereas the winters are typically cool and moist.

Each season on the island has something unique to offer travelers. The cooler moist periods are quiet and out of season, so it is ideal for visitors who which to escape the hustle and bustle of tourist hot spots. Spring is a wonderful time to visit, as the island explodes with life and songs of the nightingale. Sea temperatures can still be a little nippy this time of year though, so prepare yourself for a bracing dip, if you dare.

Be aware of the strong Tramontana wind in the northern region, especially in March, unless you are in the mood for a windy holiday. The islanders actually have names for all the winds, and harness its power as renewable energy sources.

For a live weather update, see:
http://www.holiday-weather.com/menorca/

Sightseeing Highlights

Mahon

The capital, Mahon (Mao) is a picturesque and charming little town filled with local culture by day and a pumping nightlife. The tiny streets are crammed with 18th century mansions and hide interesting shops and intimate restaurants where you can easily wile away a lazy afternoon.

The architecture is British-colonial inspired, and the oldest building, Arch de San Roque, dates back to the early 1600's.

While in Mahon, be sure to visit Placa de s'Eplanda, a very lively square over weekends. Be on the lookout for the Franco War Memorial and the original British Barracks. As it proper befitting to an ancient city, an old church completes the picture. The Church of Santa Maria is worth a visit, if only to see the massive organ with more than 3 000 pipes.

Let's not forget one of the world's largest natural harbours at a whopping three miles long, right here in Mahon. And what better way to explore the Port of Mahon than by boat?

Mahon Harbour Boat Trips

At the harbor, you can hop on one of the many traditional boats and explore the ports and coves at leisure. The Balearic Islands boasts the cleanest water found along any coast, and this is not a mere empty promise.

One of the attractive options is the Yellow Menorcan Catamarans. These boasts are impossible to miss, and will sail the full stretch of the harbour. A single trip should take up an hour and a half and will explore all the sights of the surrounding isles and forts. The guides are extremely knowledgeable and provide valuable commentary on the run. Catamarans are equipped with a well stocked bar, and a glass floor on the lower deck lets you see right to seabed.

Trips depart roughly every four minutes from the port, but they operate only during the peak seasons of April to October.

Another popular trip is the glass bottom boats from El Pirata Azul. They act as water taxis between Mahon and neighbouring towns, and also offer longer historic tours of the ports. Trips can be tailor-made according to your needs, and different fixed trips become available every day. El Pirata Azul can be contacted at 971 367 017 or alternatively at 610 904 381.

Necropolis Caves (Calas Coves)

Menorca is known for its archaeological findings, but it was the discovery of Necropolis Caves got people talking. For those with a taste of the macabre, the Necropolis Caves, commonly referred to as Calas Coves, is an absolute must see.

These caves were dug out in the rocky cliff face of the Son Domingo Gorge, and can be reached from Sant Climent. As the name so aptly suggests, the necropolis hides hundreds of ancient burial sites dating back to about 1200 BC.

There are fourteen caves in total, some of which are divided into multiple rooms and supported by columns. Tombs from the Bronze Age are easily recognizable in their basic design, while the burial chambers from the Iron Age are much more complex with pillars, doorways and even outside patios.

The most impressive of the lot are the "coves de forn" with its large underground temple and façade of motifs classic to its time.

Binibeca Beach

Recognized as the 3 kilometre stretch of unspoilt beach, Binibeca Beach lies in the Binibequer district not far from Mahon. It is mostly a residential area with a few hotels and holiday homes

Even by Menorcan standards, Binibeca is considered to be quiet. If it is pulsating nightlife and the daily bustle that you are after, give it a skip. But if you are looking for a beach to relax and soak up the surroundings, this is the place to stop at.

In Cala Torret, one of the two districts in Binebeca, there is a supermarket and several very cosy restaurants that overlook the ocean. For a place off the beaten track, the food is unpretentious but surprisingly good.

A kilometre outside of town you will find yourself in the fishing village, Binibeca Vell, which is slightly livelier, with pretty whitewashed buildings, pedestrian streets and a few more shops and restaurants than the beach area.

Mount Toro

En-route to Ciutadella from Mahon, Mount Toro dominates the skyline at 358 meters, the highest vantage point in Menorca.

A trip to this 17th century sanctuary is an absolute must for both its insight of into past and present day culture that shaped its religion and the panoramic 360 degree view of the island. On a clear day, you can even spot the neighboring island of Mallorca in the distance.

The summit is reached by a steep winding road that gradually takes you higher as the views leave you breathless. At the apex, there is an old Augustinian monastery and a modest little Renaissance church. However, the focal point is the large statue of Christ that very much reminds of Christ the Redeemer found in Rio.

Parts of the monastery are still in use today by a community of nuns, the Franciscan Sisters of Mercy. It is a place of spiritual importance, and legend states that Mount Toro got is name from the bull (toro in Spanish) which led a group of monks to a hidden statue of the Virgin Mary in the face of the rocks.

Ciutadella

Located on the temperate west coast of the island, Ciutadella is the hub of the café society, where you can take time to simply relax and watch the world go by.

It is well known for their catch of the day fresh seafood, pristine beaches and annual festivals.

The largest and most popular festival is the "Festes de Sant Ciutadella" which takes place on the 23rd and 24th of June. If you happen to find yourself in the city during this time, the festival is not to be missed. It is a lively affair, with jousting in the streets, colourful processions, horse racing and in typical Menorcan style, gin in abundance.

The city was once the capital on Menorca up to the British occupation, and the historic significance can been seen all around. In fact, the entire Old Quarter has been declared a National Historical Monument. Winding streets will let visitors discover the ancient Moor and Medieval history. The 17th century defence tower, Castell Sant Nicolas is worth a special mention, as it offers a breath-taking vantage point to see the sun set lazily over the Mediterranean

Menorca Cathedral, Ciutadella

The Menorca Cathedral in Ciutadella deserves its own entry. Originally a mosque, it was constructed as a cathedral in 1287 when Alfonso III defeated the Moors and claimed the island in the name of Christianity. It is still one of the oldest and largest buildings on the island.

Today, the style is distinctly Catalan Gothic with six chapels and numerous vaults that stir the imagination. The Chapel of Animes has a more recent Baroque influence as the cathedral changed its face in accordance with the passing centuries.

A Neo-Gothic canopy crowns the main altar, and the details, from stained glass, stone carvings and strange, mythical creatures is exquisite. In true gothic style, a large collection of gargoyles stand guard on the perimeter, and from the outside, the cathedral as quite a fortress like appearance.

Son Catlar Prehistoric Site

Son Catlar is another prehistoric site of great historical importance. What distinguishes it from the rest of the sites is the fact that is the only remaining ancient town in the Balearic Islands with its 900 meter defence wall still intact.

The settlement dates back to the Bronze Age, and was protected by series of walls and towers that survived the onslaughts of centuries. From the surrounding walls, you can see two well preserved underground rooms, one sanctuary, a cistern and five *talayots*. Talayots are large structures made of stone up to nine meters high. They are not quite unlike the pyramids we have come to know.

Son Catlar is but a short drive from Ciutadella, and is surrounded by some of the best sunbathing beaches on the island, including Cala des Talajer and Cala Macarella.

Torretrencada

Another prehistoric settlement is only seven kilometers outside Ciutadella.

Indeed, every historic settlement and every ruined town has something unique to offer travelers. At Torretrencada, you will find some of the biggest and impressive *tuala* on the island.

Tuales, meaning tables in the local dialect, are large blocks of limestone, resting on one other and carefully jointed to resemble a massive altar. Some of these tuales can weigh up to 25 tons, so this sheer engineering feat speaks of the incredible skill of their makers.

Interestingly, tuales are always found in an enclosure of other smaller buildings or constructions. The taules here are surrounded by a series of other structures, from burial caves to stone huts remnants.

San Agueda Castle

Found in the Ferreries district, San Agueda Castle was erected in the 1200's on its namesake plateau. The San Agueda hill is the third highest point on the island at 264 meters above sea-level, and it is this unobscured vantage point that made the castle a well defended fortress. It was the only stronghold to protect the island from northern invasions, and it was so successful in holding its ground that it was the last place to fall during the invasion by Alfonso III.

A rugged but still largely intact Roman Road leads up the castle where histories and cultures collide. And just like any castle worth its name, San Agueda is shrouded in myth and legend. If you are superstitious, beware.

It is said that the hill is haunted and covered in magical holes and magical traps from which you will never escape

Recommendations for the Budget Traveller

Places to Stay

Travelling to a Mediterranean paradise like Menorca can easily strain your budget when you are looking for a suitable hotel or decent lodgings. Luckily, there are quite a few privately owned comfortable hotels that won't burn through your spendings. Also don't exclude the option of private apartments and holiday homes. Often, the weekly rate per unit will work out much cheaper than a per person rate at a luxury hotel.

Hotel Mar Blava

Calle Avenida Del Mar 16, Ciutadella
0203 027 9779
http://www.hostelbookers.com/hostels/spain/menorca
/58222/
From €57 per night

Mar Blava is small intimate hotel with only 18 guestrooms, and is located in a prime location in Ciudadella. Painted in a bright pink, the hotel is hard to miss. Overlooking the water and a quiet inlet, the views are simply lovely. It is literally within walking distance of the nearest beach, with quick and easy access to the Cathedral Menorca. It is the ideal location for travellers who wish to explore the area on foot.

The hotel features a bar that overlooks the swimming pool, a restaurant and a rooftop terrace with views over the inlet, and complimentary Wi-Fi. The terrace steps give you easy access for swimming and snorkelling in the clear blue water below.

The continental breakfast includes an adequate selection of cereals, cheese, cold meats and preserves to kick start your day.

Staff are discreet and very friendly and will even assist you with planning your itinerary and tour bookings.

Hotel Hesperia Menorca Patricia

Paseo San Nicolas 90-92, Ciutadella
+34 971 385 511
http://www.hesperia.com/nh/en/hotels/spain/menorc
a/hesperia-patricia.html
From € 38 per night

Hotel Hesperia is located right next to the picturesque harbour in the historical Ciutadella. It boasts stunning views of the coast and Mediterranean Ocean, where guest can explore the many coves hidden along the shoreline, or take a refreshing dip in the sparkling clear water.

This homey hotel offers air conditioner in all the public places, but a soft sea breeze rolling in from the harbour is equally refreshing. The hotel has recently been refurbished, adding to the comfort of your stay. Bedrooms are spacious and modern, and there is a library on site, with a selection of English literature.

The swimming pool is the perfect place to sip on scrumptious cocktails while lazing in a deck chair as you soak up the sun. From its central location, you can easily explore the beautiful and historical old town on foot. The restaurant serves the three main meals a day, with an extensive children menu for the young ones.

Apartamentos Roc Lago Park

Calle Alisos s/n Cala'n Bosch, Ciutadella
+44 203 027 7155

http://www.venere.com/vacation-rentals/ciudadela/vacation-rental-roc-lago-park/
From € 27 per person per night

Roc Lago Park is offers holiday rentals comprised of various bungalows and self catering apartments in true Spanish style.

It is conveniently close to Ciutadella's city center and the sandy beaches of Cala en Bosch.

There is a wide selection of water sport excursions to pick and choose from close by, along with lively bars and an extensive entertainment program from young and old alike. There are two large outdoor swimming pools surrounded by a solarium, where you can simply can back and soak up the sun.

Hotel Globales Almirante Farragut

Urbanizacion Los Delfines, Ciutadella
01 65 69 437
http://www.hotelesglobales.com/en/club-hotel-almirante-farragut-cala-n-forcat-ciutadella-menorca.html?src=af
From €36 per night

When it comes to views and the convenience of a selection of facilities, Almirante Farragut is an excellent choice. Perched on a cliff in Cala n Forcat a short distance from the city center, the hotel overlooks the bay and inlet, providing guests with a view that is simply magnificent.

At an all inclusive package, the hotel offers excellent value for money. You will find a complete buffet in the main dining room, and there is a very spacious lounge and a few bars.

To keep guests thoroughly entertained between excursions, there are two salt water swimming pools, table tennis rooms, a tennis court, a mini club for the young ones and a variety of life shows for young and old alike. The hotel even has its very own discothèque on the grounds.

Hostal Jume

Concepción, 6, 07701 Mahón
+34 971 363 266
http://www.hostaljume.com/
info@hostaljume.com
From €18 per night

Hostal Jume is more like a guest house than a hostel, with private en-suite bathrooms and air conditioners in the rooms. It is spotlessly clean with excellent staff on hand, who provide you with fresh sheets and towels on a daily basis.

There are 39 guest rooms in total, and you can choose between single, double or quadruple rooms. The décor is simply, yet bright and airy, and continental breakfast is served in the on-site café with bread still warm from the bakery. For the price, you will be hard pressed to find lodgings of similar standards within city.

It is set in old town, and is a ten minute walk from the Santa Maria Church and Plaza de Conquesta. Jume is only 200 meters from the famous Mahon port, and guest are within walking distance of multitude of restaurants and lively bars, with the nearest beach six kilometers away.

In spite of its central location in one of the livelier parts of town, Jume is on a small quiet street across from the police station, so guest can be assured of peace and quiet when they return after an eventful day.

Places to Shop

Because Menorca is more traditional and laid back than its neighbouring islands, you shouldn't expect to do much shopping out of town, with the exception of local markets.

There are not many international chain stores here, but think of this a way to truly appreciate the local quality crafts and souvenirs.

As there are no large shopping malls, shopping is overall relaxed at a leisurely pace. Here you will only find truly unique little boutiques, so there is no repetitive shops like the mass chain stores back home.

Both Mahon and Ciutadella have fantastic open air arts and craft markets every weekend that sells a wide selection of goodies, from unique pieces of clothing to memorable souvenirs. It is worth mentioning that if you are planning to shop on a budget, it is best to avoid

Ciutadella's old town, as the prices here tend to be a little more in the high end designer category

Don't forget about the customary siesta times when you plan a shopping excursion. Usually shops close between 13.30 and 16.30 pm.

Castillo Menorca

7 Kilometers outside Ciutadella
Open between May and October from 10.00 am to 19.00 pm.

Castillo is one of the few outlet stores on the western part of the island, where you will find a few branded goods at reasonable prices and basic souvenirs. Also on offer is a fine selection of leather goods, jewellery and ceramics. The entertainment area makes this the perfect shopping and entertainment park for the entire family.

Children can let loose in the play park, featuring trampolines, swimming pools and water chutes while you go about your business unhindered.

Mercat de Claustre

Mahon Center, Clost to Carmen Church
Monday to Saturday

Markets are the best places if you are looking for a bargain, and Mercat de Claustre is no exception. The market is housed inside what used to be the convent of

Carme Cloister in the 1700's. Traders have already occupied this space for over a century. On the ground floor, you will find a selection of fresh produce, but a new addition to building added a brand new commercial space.

Here you will find a whole selection of shops that sells anything from flowers to shoes. The market provides for a great day out, and during the summer months, many cultural events and life entertainment takes place in the cloister's central space.

Centro Artesanal

Es Mercadal

Centro Artesanal in Es Mercadal town is the meeting place for artists where they can promote both modern and traditional pieces. It also showcases a wide variety of ancient trades that are still in practise to this day. This includes silversmiths, tapestry weavers and even bee keepers.

All the products can be purchased directly at the shop on the premises. Handcrafted silverware can be rather costly but goods on display can usually meet every budget. When visiting the centre, don't miss the opportunity to see master craftsman Arturo work his magic on ceramics the traditional way. A fired clay milk jug will make a great souvenir to take back home.

Bangels Accessories

Calle Angel 25, Mahon
971 354 724

As their slogan states, Bangles adds sparkles to the Mahon fashion scene. They sell an exclusive collection of well made and decently priced costume jewelry, handbags, scarves and a selection of unique accessories to prep up an old outfit.

It is a great place to shop for take-home gifts for friends and family, and your purchases will be beautifully wrapped to save you the trouble. It is also the only shop on the entire island to stock Shamballas crystal jewelry. These stylish "bling" is almost blinding in its luster.

Arts & Crafts Markets

There is no better place to find a true bargain than at an outdoor market, and luckily for you, Menorca is crawling with markets. Crawling, literally, since many of the markets belong to travelling merchants, just like times of old.

When it comes to flea market hopping, you are really spoiled for choice. Some of the most popular markets in Mahon include:

- Mercat Ambulant De S'Esplanada selling textiles and decorative goods. This market is known for travelling around.

- Mercat Ambulant del Parc Rochina stock various goods from good quality T-shirts to leather goods.

- Mercat Artesa de Mahon offers handmade goods and works of art.

Places to Eat

Eating out on a daily basis will also cost you a pretty penny and leave a hole in your pocket before you know it. Nothing is to say that you can not enjoy a daily meal in comfort at one of the many local hideouts, but the trick is to do it so wisely. Breakfast actually consist of two parts; an early morning refreshment of preserves and milky coffee, and mid morning breakfast, which is more substantial.

If you've opted for staying in a hotel, at least one of your daily meals will be included in the price. However, if you've gone the self-catering route, both cities, Mahon and Ciutadelle offer fabulous fresh food markets right in the town centers. You will also find that many restaurants and cafés offer excellent lunchtime specials.

La Minerva

Moll del Llevant 87, Mahon
97 135 1995
Main courses start at €18
Reservations required

If you like seafood, you are in for a real treat at La Minerva. It is one of Mahon's finest, and located right in the port, it is everything you will expect from an authentically Spanish eatery. The atmosphere is warm and cosy, with a mouthwatering selection of clams, mussels and lobster. For the meat lovers, there is a selection of succulent meat dishes on the menu as well, including pork loin with a plumb sauce, and mini meatballs dipped in almond sauce. In true fashion of the Med, the food is very aromatic and flavourful

The décor is relatively simple with a nautical flair and views over the harbour. All the main meals are prepared in the building across the road, and it is quite amusing to see skilled waiters dash between buildings while avoiding traffic.

Bar Restaurant España

Carrer Victori 48-50, Mahon
97 136 3299
Main Course starts at €14
Reservations are recommended, but not required

This is one of the longest continuing restaurants since it opened its doors in 1938; no small feat in this industry. The success of Espana is mostly due to the hearty portions at a very reasonable price, and a steady flow of loyal and supporting patrons. This is the place to be if you wish to rub shoulders with locals and holiday goers alike as you while away an evening in conversation.

The menu is varied to appeal to mostly everyone while naturally maintaining its distinct Spanish flair. You can expect a wide selection of seafood dishes, which will include the catch of the day, as well as meaty meals of steak, veal and pork.

Restaurante Ca Na Marga

Urb. Ses Salines n.1, Fornells
971376410
Main courses from €10
Reservations are recommended.

Located just off the Fornells highway, this family owned restaurant is unpretentious, with the sole focus on delectable food. Ca Na Marga prides itself on its authenticity, and man size steaks are cooked in the open grill in the centre of the dining room. Make no mistake; the steaks are as massive as they are succulent.

Pizzas made the traditional way are at the order of the day, but the menu is varied with a decent mixed selection.

The setting is completely casual, and there is no dress code, so it is the ideal place to stop for a bite after a long day.

Cafe Balear

Passeig Pla de Sant Joan 15, Ciutadella
+34 97 138 00 05
Main courses from €20

For over 30 years, this little piece of culinary heaven in the port of the city has been serving fresh fish caught daily by their very own boat. With main courses starting at €20 it is not the cheapest restaurant around, but it is one of the best rated restaurants in Menorca, famous for the seafood. The portions are generous, and the quality of the food is practically unsurpassable.

Aside from seafood, there is an extensive menu, with interesting dishes like the signature lobster casserole. All the desserts are home made, and the personal touch of the establishment does not go unnoticed.

La Cayena

Alaior 40, Ciutadella
971 482 212
Main courses from €8

The white washed house and the intimate interior courtyard at La Cayena will make patrons feel right at home. You can choose from an exotic menu in a very relaxed but cheerful atmosphere. The restaurant even has a selection of burgers available, something that seems to be scarcity in Menorca. If burgers are not exotic enough, the menu is further comprised of Mexican fajitas, salads, Thai and Indonesian fusion dishes, and Japanese. When you've had your fill of Mediterranean food, La Cayena is one of the best places to satisfy your taste for international cuisine.